© Armando Marichalar

Armando Marichalar
1234 Main Street
Anytown, State ZIP
Email: armandomarichalar@yahoo.com

TABLE OF CONTENTS

1. Introduction
2. Defining Success and Financial Stability
3. Setting Clear Goals
4. Investing in Education and Skill Development
5. Entrepreneurship: Navigating Risk and Reward
6. Climbing the Corporate Ladder: Strategies for Advancement
7. Harnessing the Power of Networking
8. Embracing Innovation and Adaptability
9. Financial Literacy: Managing Income and Expenses
10. Building Multiple Income Streams
11. Investing Wisely: From Stocks to Real Estate
12. Balancing Work and Life: Prioritizing Health and Relationships
13. Overcoming Challenges and Resilience
14. Case Studies: Success Stories Across Different Paths
15. Conclusion: Charting Your Course to Success

PROLOGUE

Delve into the myriad avenues individuals can pursue to achieve success and financial stability, enabling them to support themselves and their families. Through a blend of practical advice, psychological insights, and case studies, it offers a comprehensive roadmap for personal and professional growth.

1. INTRODUCTION: ESTABLISHES THE SIGNIFICANCE OF ACHIEVING SUCCESS AND FINANCIAL STABILITY, SETTING THE STAGE FOR THE SUBSEQUENT EXPLORATION.

Introduction:

In the intricate tapestry of human existence, the quest for success and financial stability stands as a timeless pursuit. Embedded within this pursuit are layers of aspirations, motivations, and societal constructs that shape individuals' perceptions and actions. Chapter 1 serves as the foundational cornerstone upon which the subsequent exploration of success and financial stability is erected. It illuminates the nuanced definitions, intrinsic values, and overarching significance of these concepts, paving the way for a deeper understanding of the pathways to achievement.

Defining Success and Financial Stability:

At the heart of the human experience lies the quest for success—a concept as diverse and multifaceted as the individuals who pursue it. While commonly associated with material wealth and career accomplishments, success transcends these conventional markers. It encompasses personal growth, fulfillment in relationships, contribution to society, and alignment with one's values and passions. Success, therefore, becomes a deeply personal journey, shaped by individual aspirations, cultural influences, and societal expectations.

Financial stability, inseparable from the pursuit of success, forms the bedrock upon which individuals can build their lives and pursue their dreams. Beyond the mere accumulation of wealth, financial stability embodies security, resilience, and the ability to navigate life's uncertainties. It encompasses prudent financial management, the cultivation of multiple income streams, and the capacity to weather economic fluctuations without compromising one's well-being.

Beyond Material Wealth:

While material wealth undoubtedly plays a significant role in societal perceptions of success, true fulfillment extends beyond the confines of monetary abundance. Success, in its purest form, encompasses emotional well-being, mental resilience, and a sense of purpose that transcends material possessions. It is found in the richness of human connections, the pursuit of passions, and the fulfillment derived from making a positive impact on the world.

In today's hyperconnected world, where the pursuit of success often intersects with relentless ambition and unyielding competition, it becomes imperative to reframe our understanding of success. It is not merely a destination to be reached but a journey to be savored—a journey marked by growth, self-discovery, and the pursuit of happiness in its myriad forms.

The Pursuit of Happiness:

Ultimately, the pursuit of success and financial stability is intricately intertwined with the pursuit of happiness. It is about crafting a life that aligns with one's values, passions, and innate desires—a life that brings joy, fulfillment, and a sense of purpose.

Happiness, as the ultimate currency of human existence, becomes the guiding compass that steers individuals along their respective paths.

In a world characterized by rapid change, uncertainty, and evolving societal norms, the pursuit of happiness emerges as the cornerstone of human flourishing. It entails cultivating resilience in the face of adversity, fostering meaningful relationships, and embracing the impermanence of life with grace and acceptance.

As we embark on this odyssey of exploration into the realms of success and financial stability, it becomes increasingly evident that these concepts are not static constructs but dynamic manifestations of human ingenuity and aspiration. Success, in its myriad forms, beckons individuals to embark on a journey of self-discovery, growth, and fulfillment—a journey that transcends the boundaries of material wealth and societal acclaim.

Financial stability, as the enabler of this journey, provides the necessary foundation upon which individuals can build their dreams and aspirations. It is the scaffolding that supports their endeavors, shields them from life's uncertainties, and empowers them to chart their course with confidence and conviction.

In the chapters that follow, we will delve deeper into the practical strategies, psychological insights, and real-world examples that illuminate the path to success and financial stability. Through introspection, exploration, and a steadfast commitment to personal growth, readers will be equipped with the tools and perspectives necessary to navigate the complexities of modern life and embark on their own journeys of fulfillment and prosperity.

"HUMAN EXPERIENCE LIES THE QUEST FOR SUCCESS."

2. DEFINING SUCCESS AND FINANCIAL STABILITY: EXPLORES THE MULTIFACETED NATURE OF SUCCESS BEYOND MONETARY WEALTH, EMPHASIZING THE IMPORTANCE OF HOLISTIC WELL-BEING.

In the intricate landscape of human ambition, success and financial stability stand as towering pillars upon which individuals build their aspirations and dreams. Chapter 2 delves deep into the essence of these concepts, unraveling their multifaceted nature and illuminating their significance in the pursuit of a fulfilling life.

The Multifaceted Nature of Success:

Success, often portrayed as the pinnacle of achievement, transcends the boundaries of conventional metrics such as wealth and status. It encompasses a kaleidoscope of dimensions, each contributing to an individual's sense of fulfillment and purpose. While career accomplishments and financial prosperity form integral components of success, they are but fragments of a larger mosaic.

Success, in its purest form, encompasses personal growth, meaningful relationships, and the pursuit of passions that ignite the soul. It is found in the small victories of everyday life, the resilience forged in the face of adversity, and the courage to chart one's own path against the currents of societal expectations.

Financial Stability: The Foundation of Prosperity:

At the cornerstone of the pursuit of success lies financial stability — a sturdy foundation upon which individuals can build their dreams and aspirations. Financial stability, far from being a static state, embodies the principles of prudence, resilience, and foresight. It entails the ability to manage one's finances judiciously, navigate economic uncertainties, and plan for the future with confidence.

Financial stability is not merely about amassing wealth but about cultivating a mindset of abundance and security. It involves living within one's means, saving for emergencies, and investing in assets that yield long-term returns. By fostering financial stability, individuals can liberate themselves from the shackles of financial insecurity and embark on their journeys with a sense of purpose and freedom.

Redefining Success in the Modern Era:

In an age defined by rapid technological advancements and shifting societal norms, the traditional notions of success are undergoing a profound transformation. The rise of the gig economy, remote work, and digital entrepreneurship has expanded the horizons of success, offering individuals unprecedented opportunities to redefine their paths on their own terms.

Success, in the modern era, is not confined to the confines of a corner office or a nine-to-five job. It is found in the flexibility to pursue multiple passions, the autonomy to design one's own work-life balance, and the freedom to explore unconventional career trajectories. By embracing this fluidity, individuals can chart their courses with creativity, resilience, and a spirit of adventure.

Financial Stability as a Catalyst for Personal Growth:

While financial stability is often viewed as an end in itself, it serves as a powerful catalyst for personal growth and self-actualization. When individuals are freed from the burdens of financial insecurity, they can devote their energies to pursuits that enrich their lives and contribute to the greater good.

Financial stability provides the resources and stability necessary to pursue education, invest in skill development, and explore entrepreneurial ventures. It empowers individuals to take calculated risks, pursue their passions, and leverage their talents to create value in the world. By cultivating financial stability, individuals can unleash their full potential and embark on a journey of continuous growth and self-discovery.

In conclusion, success and financial stability are not mere destinations to be reached but ongoing journeys of self-discovery, growth, and fulfillment. By embracing the multifaceted nature of success, redefining traditional notions of achievement, and cultivating financial stability as a catalyst for personal growth, individuals can unlock the doors to a life of abundance, purpose, and prosperity. In the chapters that follow, we will delve deeper into the practical strategies, psychological insights, and real-world examples that illuminate the path to success and financial stability, empowering readers to embark on their own journeys with confidence and conviction.

"FINANCIAL STABILITY IS NOT MERELY ABOUT AMASSING WEALTH BUT ABOUT CULTIVATING A MINDSET OF ABUNDANCE AND SECURITY."

3. SETTING CLEAR GOALS: DISCUSSES THE NECESSITY OF SETTING SPECIFIC, MEASURABLE, ACHIEVABLE, RELEVANT, AND TIME-BOUND (SMART) GOALS TO GUIDE ONE'S JOURNEY.

Goals serve as the compass guiding individuals through the labyrinth of life, providing direction, purpose, and motivation. Chapter 3 delves into the intricacies of goal setting, exploring the art and science behind this fundamental practice and its indispensable role in the pursuit of success and financial stability.

Understanding the Power of Goals:

Goals are more than mere aspirations; they are concrete manifestations of one's desires, dreams, and ambitions. By defining clear, specific objectives, individuals create a roadmap for their journey, delineating the steps needed to turn their visions into reality. Goals provide focus, clarity, and a sense of purpose, empowering individuals to channel their efforts toward meaningful outcomes.

The Importance of Clarity and Specificity:

Clarity is the cornerstone of effective goal setting. Vague, nebulous objectives lack the precision needed to guide action and measure progress. Specificity, on the other hand, provides a clear target for individuals to aim for, enabling them to break down complex aspirations into manageable tasks and milestones.

The SMART Goal Framework:

The SMART goal framework—a widely recognized approach to goal setting—provides a blueprint for creating clear, actionable objectives. SMART goals are Specific, Measurable, Achievable, Relevant, and Time-bound. By adhering to these criteria, individuals ensure that their goals are well-defined, attainable, and aligned with their broader aspirations.

Setting Short-term and Long-term Goals:

Effective goal setting involves striking a balance between short-term objectives and long-term aspirations. Short-term goals provide immediate targets for action, fostering momentum and progress in the present moment. Long-term goals, on the other hand, provide a sense of direction and purpose, guiding individuals toward their overarching vision of success.

The Power of Visualization and Affirmation:

Visualization and affirmation serve as powerful tools for goal setting, harnessing the power of the mind to manifest desired outcomes. By vividly imagining oneself achieving their goals and affirming their capabilities and worthiness, individuals prime their subconscious minds for success, aligning their thoughts, beliefs, and actions with their aspirations.

Overcoming Challenges and Maintaining Motivation:

The path to achieving goals is rarely linear; it is fraught with obstacles, setbacks, and moments of doubt. Effective goal setting involves anticipating challenges and developing strategies to overcome them. By cultivating resilience, perseverance, and a growth mindset, individuals can navigate setbacks with grace and determination, using each obstacle as an opportunity for learning and growth.

Reviewing and Adjusting Goals as Needed:

Goal setting is an iterative process, requiring ongoing reflection, review, and adjustment. As circumstances change and new information emerges, individuals may need to recalibrate their goals to ensure they remain relevant and aligned with their evolving aspirations. Regular check-ins and progress assessments enable individuals to stay on track and make informed decisions about their priorities and actions. Goal setting is a foundational practice in the pursuit of success and financial stability. By defining clear, specific objectives and adhering to the principles of clarity, specificity, and relevance, individuals can create a roadmap for their journey, guiding their actions and decisions with purpose and intention. Through visualization, affirmation, and resilience, individuals can overcome challenges, maintain motivation, and stay focused on their goals, even in the face of adversity. In the chapters that follow, we will delve deeper into the practical strategies, psychological insights, and real-world examples that illuminate the path to success and financial stability, empowering readers to set and achieve their goals with confidence and conviction.

"GOAL SETTING IS A FOUNDATIONAL PRACTICE IN THE PURSUIT OF SUCCESS AND FINANCIAL STABILITY."

4. INVESTING IN EDUCATION AND SKILL DEVELOPMENT: ADVOCATES FOR LIFELONG LEARNING AND SKILL ENHANCEMENT AS KEY DRIVERS OF PERSONAL AND PROFESSIONAL GROWTH.

In today's rapidly evolving world, the pursuit of success and financial stability hinges upon one's ability to adapt, innovate, and stay ahead of the curve. Chapter 4 delves into the transformative power of education and skill development, exploring how lifelong learning serves as a cornerstone for personal and professional growth.

The Imperative of Lifelong Learning:

Education is not a destination but a journey—a continuous process of growth and evolution that spans the entirety of one's life. In an era marked by technological disruption and shifting economic landscapes, the imperative of lifelong learning has never been greater. By embracing a mindset of curiosity and intellectual curiosity, individuals can unlock new opportunities, expand their horizons, and remain relevant in an ever-changing world.

The Benefits of Education and Skill Development:

Investing in education and skill development yields dividends that extend far beyond the confines of the classroom. It equips individuals with the knowledge, expertise, and competencies needed to thrive in today's knowledge-based economy. From acquiring new technical skills to honing critical thinking and problem-solving abilities, education empowers individuals to navigate complex challenges, seize opportunities, and chart their own paths to success.

Formal Education vs. Informal Learning:

While formal education plays a crucial role in laying the foundation for academic and professional success, it is but one facet of the broader landscape of learning. Informal learning—through self-study, online courses, workshops, and mentorship—offers a wealth of opportunities for individuals to deepen their expertise, explore new interests, and stay abreast of emerging trends. By embracing a holistic approach to learning, individuals can blend formal education with informal experiences to cultivate a well-rounded skill set that transcends traditional boundaries.

Navigating the Digital Learning Landscape:

The advent of digital technologies has revolutionized the way we access and consume educational content, democratizing learning and expanding access to knowledge on a global scale. Online platforms, such as Coursera, Udemy, and Khan Academy, offer a vast array of courses covering everything from technical skills to personal development and entrepreneurship. By harnessing the power of digital learning, individuals can tailor their educational experiences to their unique needs and preferences, learning at their own pace and on their own terms.

The Role of Skill Development in Career Advancement:

In today's competitive job market, possessing technical skills alone is no longer sufficient to secure employment and advance in one's career. Employers increasingly value a diverse skill set that encompasses not only technical proficiency but also soft skills such as communication, teamwork, and adaptability. By investing in skill development, individuals can position themselves as valuable assets in the workplace, enhancing their employability and opening doors to new opportunities for advancement and growth.

In conclusion, investing in education and skill development is a strategic imperative for individuals seeking to achieve success and financial stability in today's fast-paced world. By embracing a lifelong learning mindset, individuals can unlock their full potential, adapt to changing circumstances, and seize opportunities for personal and professional growth. In the chapters that follow, we will delve deeper into the practical strategies, resources, and real-world examples that illuminate the path to success through education and skill development, empowering readers to embark on their own journeys of lifelong learning with confidence and conviction.

"IN TODAY'S COMPETITIVE JOB MARKET, POSSESSING TECHNICAL SKILLS ALONE IS NO LONGER SUFFICIENT TO SECURE EMPLOYMENT AND ADVANCE IN ONE'S CAREER."

5. ENTREPRENEURSHIP: EXPLORES THE ENTREPRENEURIAL MINDSET, RISK MANAGEMENT STRATEGIES, AND THE PATH TO BUILDING SUCCESSFUL VENTURES.

Entrepreneurship stands as a beacon of innovation, creativity, and possibility in the modern world. Chapter 5 delves into the dynamic realm of entrepreneurship, exploring the intricacies of venturing into the unknown, navigating risks, and reaping the rewards of entrepreneurial endeavor.

The Entrepreneurial Spirit:

At its core, entrepreneurship embodies the spirit of ingenuity, resilience, and audacity—the willingness to challenge the status quo, disrupt industries, and create value where none existed before. Entrepreneurs are visionaries, trailblazers who dare to dream big, defy convention, and carve their own paths in pursuit of success and fulfillment.

Embracing Risk and Uncertainty:

Entrepreneurship is inherently fraught with risk and uncertainty—a high-stakes game where success and failure often hang in the balance. Yet, it is precisely this element of risk that fuels the entrepreneurial spirit, driving individuals to push beyond their comfort zones, embrace uncertainty, and seize opportunities where others see obstacles.

The Entrepreneurial Mindset:

At the heart of entrepreneurship lies a mindset characterized by creativity, adaptability, and a relentless drive to innovate. Entrepreneurs are problem-solvers, constantly seeking out new ways to address unmet needs, capitalize on emerging trends, and create value for their customers. They possess a keen sense of curiosity, an appetite for experimentation, and an unwavering belief in their ability to effect meaningful change in the world.

Navigating the Startup Journey:

The journey of entrepreneurship is marked by highs and lows, triumphs and setbacks, moments of exhilaration and periods of doubt. From conceiving a groundbreaking idea to bringing it to market, entrepreneurs must navigate a complex maze of challenges, from securing funding and building a team to scaling operations and navigating regulatory hurdles. Yet, it is precisely these obstacles that serve as the crucible in which entrepreneurs forge their character, refine their vision, and ultimately realize their dreams.

The Role of Innovation and Adaptability:

Innovation lies at the heart of entrepreneurship, driving individuals to push the boundaries of what is possible, challenge conventional wisdom, and pioneer new ways of doing business. Yet, innovation alone is not enough; entrepreneurs must also possess the agility and adaptability to pivot in response to changing market conditions, customer preferences, and competitive dynamics. By embracing a culture of continuous learning and experimentation, entrepreneurs can stay ahead of the curve, capitalize on emerging opportunities, and sustain long-term growth and success.

Building a Sustainable Business Model:

While vision and creativity are essential components of entrepreneurship, they must be grounded in a solid foundation of business acumen, strategic planning, and financial management. Entrepreneurs must develop a clear value proposition, identify their target market, and devise a sustainable business model that enables them to generate revenue, manage costs, and deliver value to their customers. By focusing on building a strong foundation, entrepreneurs can create businesses that are not only innovative but also resilient, adaptable, and positioned for long-term success.

Entrepreneurship represents a bold and transformative path to success and financial stability—one characterized by innovation, risk-taking, and the relentless pursuit of opportunity. By embracing the entrepreneurial spirit, individuals can challenge the status quo, defy convention, and create value in ways that have the power to transform industries, communities, and lives. In the chapters that follow, we will delve deeper into the practical strategies, resources, and real-world examples that illuminate the path to success through entrepreneurship, empowering readers to embark on their own entrepreneurial journeys with confidence and conviction.

"ENTREPRENEURSHIP EMBODIES THE SPIRIT OF INGENUITY, RESILIENCE, AND AUDACITY—THE WILLINGNESS TO CHALLENGE THE STATUS QUO, DISRUPT INDUSTRIES, AND CREATE VALUE WHERE NONE EXISTED BEFORE."

6. CLIMBING THE CORPORATE LADDER: EXAMINES STRATEGIES FOR CAREER ADVANCEMENT WITHIN ORGANIZATIONAL SETTINGS, INCLUDING LEADERSHIP DEVELOPMENT AND STRATEGIC NETWORKING.

Within the structured confines of corporate environments, the pursuit of success and financial stability often takes the form of climbing the proverbial corporate ladder. Chapter 6 delves into the intricacies of navigating corporate hierarchies, advancing one's career, and achieving prosperity through strategic planning and deliberate action.

Understanding Corporate Dynamics:

Corporate environments are complex ecosystems governed by hierarchies, politics, and unwritten rules of engagement. Success within these environments requires a nuanced understanding of organizational dynamics, including power structures, decision-making processes, and cultural norms. By deciphering these dynamics, individuals can position themselves strategically, identify opportunities for advancement, and leverage their strengths to achieve their career aspirations.

Setting Career Goals and Objectives:

At the heart of career advancement lies the art of goal setting—a process that involves defining clear, actionable objectives, and charting a path to achieve them. Whether aiming for a promotion, seeking to expand one's skill set, or aspiring to take on new responsibilities, setting career goals provides a roadmap for success and a framework for measuring progress. By aligning their career goals with their personal aspirations and the strategic priorities of the organization, individuals can create a compelling case for advancement and demonstrate their value as high-performing professionals.

Building Strategic Relationships:

In corporate environments, success is often as much about who you know as what you know. Building strategic relationships with key stakeholders, mentors, and influencers can play a pivotal role in advancing one's career. By cultivating a strong network of allies and advocates, individuals can gain access to opportunities, receive valuable feedback and guidance, and position themselves as trusted advisors and collaborators within the organization.

Demonstrating Leadership Potential:

Leadership skills are highly valued in corporate environments, as they signal an individual's ability to inspire, influence, and drive results. By demonstrating leadership potential through initiatives such as taking on leadership roles in cross-functional projects, mentoring junior colleagues, or spearheading innovative initiatives, individuals can differentiate themselves from their peers and position themselves for advancement into leadership roles.

Continuous Learning and Skill Development:

In today's fast-paced business landscape, the only constant is change. To remain competitive and relevant in their careers, individuals must commit to lifelong learning and skill development. By pursuing opportunities for professional development, such as attending industry conferences, enrolling in training programs, or pursuing advanced degrees or certifications, individuals can enhance their expertise, expand their skill set, and stay ahead of the curve in their respective fields.

Navigating Organizational Politics:

Corporate environments are not immune to office politics—a complex web of power struggles, competing interests, and hidden agendas. Navigating these dynamics requires a delicate balance of diplomacy, tact, and strategic maneuvering. By staying informed, building alliances, and maintaining a positive reputation, individuals can navigate organizational politics effectively, mitigate risks, and advance their careers with integrity and professionalism.

Climbing the corporate ladder requires a combination of strategic planning, relationship building, and continuous learning. By understanding corporate dynamics, setting clear career goals, building strategic relationships, demonstrating leadership potential, and navigating organizational politics with finesse, individuals can position themselves for success and advancement within their organizations. In the chapters that follow, we will delve deeper into the practical strategies, resources, and real-world examples that illuminate the path to success within corporate environments, empowering readers to navigate their careers with confidence and purpose.

"TO REMAIN COMPETITIVE AND RELEVANT IN THEIR CAREERS, INDIVIDUALS MUST COMMIT TO LIFELONG LEARNING AND SKILL DEVELOPMENT."

7. HARNESSING THE POWER OF NETWORKING: HIGHLIGHTS THE IMPORTANCE OF CULTIVATING MEANINGFUL CONNECTIONS AND LEVERAGING NETWORKS TO ACCESS OPPORTUNITIES.

Networking stands as a cornerstone of professional success, offering individuals the opportunity to forge connections, cultivate relationships, and unlock new opportunities for advancement. Chapter 7 delves into the transformative power of networking, exploring the strategies, techniques, and benefits of building and nurturing a strong professional network.

Understanding the Essence of Networking:

At its core, networking is about more than just exchanging business cards or collecting LinkedIn connections—it's about building genuine, mutually beneficial relationships with individuals who share common interests, goals, or values. Networking encompasses a spectrum of activities, from attending industry events and conferences to participating in online forums and engaging in one-on-one conversations. By cultivating a diverse network of contacts, individuals can tap into a wealth of resources, insights, and opportunities that can propel their careers forward.

The Importance of Authenticity and Genuine Connection:

Effective networking is rooted in authenticity and genuine connection. Rather than approaching networking as a transactional exercise aimed solely at advancing one's own interests, individuals should focus on building meaningful relationships based on trust, respect, and mutual support. By demonstrating authenticity, empathy, and a genuine interest in others, individuals can foster deeper connections that endure beyond superficial interactions.

Strategies for Successful Networking:

Successful networking requires a strategic approach that balances quantity with quality. Rather than casting a wide net and collecting a large number of contacts, individuals should focus on nurturing a smaller, more meaningful network of relationships. This involves identifying key individuals within their industry or field of interest, actively engaging with them, and providing value through knowledge sharing, introductions, or collaborative opportunities.

Utilizing Online and Offline Networking Channels:

Networking opportunities abound in both online and offline environments, offering individuals a variety of channels through which to connect with others. Online platforms such as LinkedIn, Twitter, and professional forums provide a convenient way to expand one's network and engage with like-minded professionals from around the world. Offline events such as conferences, workshops, and industry meetups offer valuable opportunities for face-to-face interaction and relationship building. By leveraging both online and offline networking channels, individuals can maximize their reach and visibility within their professional communities.

The Power of Reciprocity and Giving Back:

Networking is a two-way street, and successful relationships are built on a foundation of reciprocity and mutual support. Rather than focusing solely on what they can gain from their network, individuals should seek opportunities to give back and support others in their professional journeys. This might involve offering mentorship to junior colleagues, making introductions between contacts, or sharing valuable insights and resources. By cultivating a culture of generosity and reciprocity within their network, individuals can strengthen their relationships and foster a community of collaboration and mutual growth.

Overcoming Networking Challenges and Building Confidence:

For many individuals, networking can be daunting, particularly for introverts or those new to their industry. Overcoming networking challenges requires building confidence, developing effective communication skills, and adopting a growth mindset. By setting achievable goals, practicing active listening, and seeking out opportunities for exposure and practice, individuals can gradually build their networking skills and become more comfortable engaging with others in professional settings.

Networking is a powerful tool for professional advancement, offering individuals the opportunity to forge connections, cultivate relationships, and unlock new opportunities for growth and success. By approaching networking with authenticity, strategic intent, and a spirit of reciprocity, individuals can build a strong professional network that serves as a source of support, inspiration, and opportunity throughout their careers. In the chapters that follow, we will delve deeper into the practical strategies, resources, and real-world examples that illuminate the path to successful networking, empowering readers to cultivate strong professional relationships and thrive in their professional endeavors.

"NETWORKING IS A POWERFUL TOOL FOR PROFESSIONAL ADVANCEMENT, OFFERING INDIVIDUALS THE OPPORTUNITY TO FORGE CONNECTIONS, CULTIVATE RELATIONSHIPS, AND UNLOCK NEW OPPORTUNITIES FOR GROWTH AND SUCCESS."

8. EMBRACING INNOVATION AND ADAPTABILITY: DISCUSSES THE ROLE OF INNOVATION, CREATIVITY, AND ADAPTABILITY IN NAVIGATING DYNAMIC CAREER LANDSCAPES.

Innovation and adaptability are the twin engines that drive progress and success in today's rapidly evolving world. Chapter 8 explores the transformative power of innovation and adaptability, illuminating the strategies, mindsets, and practices that enable individuals to thrive amidst change and uncertainty.

The Imperative of Innovation:

Innovation lies at the heart of human progress, fueling advancements in technology, science, business, and society. At its essence, innovation involves the creation of new ideas, products, or processes that deliver value and drive positive change. In an era marked by relentless disruption and competition, the ability to innovate has become a critical differentiator for individuals seeking to stay ahead of the curve and seize new opportunities for growth and success.

Fostering a Culture of Creativity:

Creativity is the lifeblood of innovation, empowering individuals to generate novel ideas, challenge the status quo, and envision new possibilities. Fostering a culture of creativity involves creating an environment that encourages experimentation, embraces failure as a natural part of the learning process, and celebrates diversity of thought and perspective. By cultivating a culture of creativity within their organizations and communities, individuals can unlock the full potential of their teams and unleash a torrent of innovation that propels them forward.

The Role of Adaptability in Navigating Change:

Adaptability is the ability to respond effectively to changing circumstances, environments, or demands. In today's fast-paced world, characterized by rapid technological advancements, shifting market dynamics, and unpredictable global events, adaptability has become a prerequisite for survival and success. Individuals who possess the capacity to adapt can thrive amidst uncertainty, pivot in response to new challenges, and seize emerging opportunities with agility and resilience.

Embracing a Growth Mindset:

Central to both innovation and adaptability is the concept of a growth mindset—the belief that intelligence, abilities, and talents can be developed through effort, perseverance, and learning. Individuals with a growth mindset embrace challenges as opportunities for growth, view failure as a temporary setback, and seek out feedback and criticism as avenues for improvement. By cultivating a growth mindset, individuals can overcome self-limiting beliefs, unleash their full potential, and embrace change as a catalyst for personal and professional growth.

Navigating Disruption and Seizing Opportunities:

Disruption is a natural and inevitable part of the innovation process, as new technologies, business models, and market entrants disrupt established norms and paradigms. Rather than viewing disruption as a threat, individuals can seize it as an opportunity to innovate, adapt, and reinvent themselves and their organizations. By staying attuned to emerging trends, embracing experimentation, and remaining open to new ideas and perspectives, individuals can position themselves to capitalize on disruptive forces and drive meaningful change in their industries and communities.

Creating a Future-ready Mindset:

As the pace of change accelerates and the forces of disruption intensify, individuals must cultivate a future-ready mindset—a mindset characterized by curiosity, resilience, and a willingness to embrace uncertainty. By adopting a proactive approach to learning, staying abreast of emerging technologies and trends, and continuously challenging themselves to push beyond their comfort zones, individuals can future-proof their careers and position themselves as leaders and innovators in their fields.

Innovation and adaptability are twin pillars of success in today's dynamic and uncertain world. By fostering a culture of creativity, embracing a growth mindset, and staying attuned to emerging trends and opportunities, individuals can unlock their full potential, navigate change with confidence, and thrive amidst uncertainty. In the chapters that follow, we will delve deeper into the practical strategies, resources, and real-world examples that illuminate the path to success through innovation and adaptability, empowering readers to embrace change as a catalyst for growth and transformation.

"IN AN ERA MARKED BY RELENTLESS DISRUPTION AND COMPETITION, THE ABILITY TO INNOVATE HAS BECOME A CRITICAL DIFFERENTIATOR FOR INDIVIDUALS SEEKING TO STAY AHEAD OF THE CURVE AND SEIZE NEW OPPORTUNITIES FOR GROWTH AND SUCCESS."

9. FINANCIAL LITERACY: PROVIDES PRACTICAL INSIGHTS INTO MANAGING FINANCES, BUDGETING, SAVING, AND AVOIDING DEBT TRAPS.

Financial literacy is the cornerstone of personal finance, empowering individuals to make informed decisions about their money and achieve their financial goals. At the heart of financial literacy lies the ability to manage income and expenses effectively, ensuring that earnings are maximized, debts are minimized, and resources are allocated wisely. In this chapter, we delve into the principles, strategies, and practices of managing income and expenses, equipping readers with the knowledge and tools needed to build a solid financial foundation and achieve long-term financial security.

Understanding Income and Expenses:

Income represents the money that individuals earn from various sources, including salaries, wages, investments, and business ventures. Expenses, on the other hand, are the costs incurred to meet one's needs and desires, including housing, food, transportation, utilities, debt payments, and discretionary spending. Effective financial management involves optimizing income, minimizing expenses, and ensuring that resources are allocated in alignment with one's financial goals and priorities.

Creating a Budget:

A budget serves as a roadmap for financial success, providing a framework for tracking income and expenses, identifying areas for savings, and setting goals for spending and saving. To create a budget, individuals should start by listing their sources of income and estimating their monthly expenses in various categories. By comparing income to expenses and making adjustments as needed, individuals can create a budget that reflects their financial reality and helps them achieve their short-term and long-term financial goals.

Differentiating Between Needs and Wants:

A fundamental aspect of managing expenses is differentiating between needs and wants. Needs are essential expenses that are necessary for survival and well-being, such as housing, food, healthcare, and transportation. Wants, on the other hand, are non-essential expenses that are desirable but not strictly necessary for survival, such as entertainment, dining out, and luxury items. By prioritizing needs over wants and making conscious choices about discretionary spending, individuals can ensure that their resources are allocated in a way that supports their financial goals and priorities.

Tracking Spending and Identifying Areas for Savings:

Tracking spending is a critical step in managing expenses effectively, as it provides insight into where money is being spent and highlights opportunities for savings. This can be done using various methods, including budgeting apps, spreadsheets, or pen and paper. By reviewing spending patterns and identifying areas where expenses can be reduced or eliminated, individuals can free up resources to allocate towards savings goals, debt repayment, or other financial priorities.

Building an Emergency Fund:

An emergency fund is a crucial component of financial stability, providing a financial safety net to cover unexpected expenses or income disruptions. Financial experts recommend setting aside three to six months' worth of living expenses in an easily accessible savings account. By prioritizing savings and contributing regularly to an emergency fund, individuals can protect themselves from financial hardship and weather unexpected challenges with confidence and peace of mind.

Managing Debt Wisely:

Debt can be a double-edged sword, providing access to resources and opportunities while also posing risks to financial stability if not managed responsibly. Effective debt management involves minimizing high-interest debt, such as credit card debt, and prioritizing debt repayment strategies, such as the debt snowball or debt avalanche method. By reducing debt burden and avoiding unnecessary borrowing, individuals can free up resources to allocate towards savings, investments, or other financial goals.

Increasing Income Through Additional Sources:

In addition to managing expenses, individuals can increase their overall financial resilience by seeking out additional sources of income. This may involve exploring opportunities for side hustles, freelance work, rental income, or passive investments such as dividend-paying stocks or real estate. By diversifying sources of income, individuals can increase their earning potential, reduce reliance on a single income stream, and create opportunities for financial growth and prosperity.

Seeking Professional Advice:

For individuals facing complex financial situations or struggling to manage income and expenses effectively, seeking professional financial advice can be invaluable. Financial advisors can provide personalized guidance, tailored recommendations, and actionable strategies to help individuals achieve their financial goals and navigate challenges such as debt management, retirement planning, or investment strategies. By leveraging the expertise of financial professionals, individuals can gain confidence and clarity in their financial decisions and work towards a brighter financial future.

Managing income and expenses effectively is a fundamental aspect of financial literacy and personal finance. By creating a budget, differentiating between needs and wants, tracking spending, building an emergency fund, managing debt wisely, increasing income through additional sources, and seeking professional advice when needed, individuals can take control of their finances, achieve their financial goals, and build a secure and prosperous future. In the chapters that follow, we will delve deeper into the principles, strategies, and practices of financial literacy, empowering readers to make informed decisions about their money and achieve financial success and well-being.

"BY REDUCING DEBT BURDEN AND AVOIDING UNNECESSARY BORROWING, INDIVIDUALS CAN FREE UP RESOURCES TO ALLOCATE TOWARDS SAVINGS, INVESTMENTS, OR OTHER FINANCIAL GOALS."

10. BUILDING MULTIPLE INCOME STREAMS: EXPLORES THE CONCEPT OF DIVERSIFYING INCOME SOURCES TO ENHANCE FINANCIAL STABILITY AND RESILIENCE.

In today's dynamic and uncertain economic landscape, the concept of relying solely on a single source of income for financial security is increasingly outdated and risky. Instead, individuals are recognizing the importance of building multiple income streams as a means of diversifying risk, increasing financial stability, and enhancing resilience in the face of unforeseen challenges. This chapter delves into the transformative power of building multiple income streams, exploring the principles, strategies, and benefits of diversifying income sources to achieve long-term financial success and well-being.

Understanding Multiple Income Streams:

Multiple income streams refer to the concept of generating revenue from various sources, rather than relying solely on a single source of income such as a full-time job. These income streams can take various forms, including employment income, passive income from investments, rental income from real estate, income from side businesses or freelancing, royalties from intellectual property, and dividends from stocks or mutual funds. By diversifying income sources, individuals can reduce reliance on any single source of income and create a more resilient financial portfolio.

Diversifying Risk and Increasing Stability:

One of the key benefits of building multiple income streams is the ability to diversify risk and increase financial stability. Relying solely on a single source of income leaves individuals vulnerable to unexpected events such as job loss, economic downturns, or industry disruptions. By diversifying income sources across various streams, individuals can spread risk and mitigate the impact of unforeseen challenges on their overall financial well-being. Even if one income stream is temporarily disrupted, others can continue to generate revenue, providing a buffer against financial hardship and ensuring continuity of income.

Creating Redundancy and Security:

Building multiple income streams creates redundancy in one's financial portfolio, providing a safety net in the event of unexpected setbacks or emergencies. Rather than relying solely on a single paycheck to cover living expenses, individuals with multiple income streams have additional sources of revenue to fall back on during times of need. This redundancy provides a sense of security and peace of mind, knowing that there are multiple avenues for generating income and supporting oneself and one's family, even in challenging circumstances.

Unlocking Financial Freedom and Flexibility:

Building multiple income streams can also unlock greater financial freedom and flexibility, allowing individuals to design lifestyles that align with their values, priorities, and goals. With multiple income streams, individuals may have the flexibility to pursue passion projects, take career breaks, travel, or spend more time with family without worrying about financial constraints. This freedom empowers individuals to live life on their own terms, pursue their dreams, and achieve a greater sense of fulfillment and well-being.

Maximizing Earning Potential:

Diversifying income sources also enables individuals to maximize their earning potential and increase overall income levels. While a full-time job may provide a steady paycheck, additional income streams offer opportunities to supplement earnings and boost total income. Whether through side businesses, freelance work, rental properties, or investments, individuals can leverage multiple income streams to increase cash flow, accelerate savings, and achieve financial goals such as homeownership, retirement, or financial independence.

Embracing Entrepreneurship and Innovation:

Building multiple income streams often involves embracing entrepreneurship and innovation, as individuals explore new opportunities for generating revenue outside of traditional employment channels. Side businesses, freelance work, and other entrepreneurial ventures offer avenues for creativity, self-expression, and financial growth. By tapping into their skills, passions, and talents, individuals can create value for others, solve problems, and capitalize on emerging trends to build successful and sustainable income streams.

Investing for Passive Income:

Passive income streams, such as dividends from stocks, interest from bonds, or rental income from real estate, offer a particularly attractive avenue for building multiple income streams. Unlike active income, which requires ongoing effort and time investment, passive income can be generated with minimal ongoing involvement once the initial investment has been made. By investing strategically in income-generating assets, individuals can create a steady stream of passive income that continues to grow and compound over time, providing financial security and peace of mind.

Building multiple income streams is a powerful strategy for enhancing financial stability, resilience, and well-being. By diversifying income sources, individuals can spread risk, increase stability, unlock financial freedom, maximize earning potential, embrace entrepreneurship, and invest for passive income. Whether through employment, entrepreneurship, investments, or other means, building multiple income streams empowers individuals to take control of their finances, achieve their goals, and create a more secure and prosperous future for themselves and their families. In the chapters that follow, we will delve deeper into the principles, strategies, and practical steps for building multiple income streams, empowering readers to take charge of their financial destinies and achieve lasting financial success and well-being.

"PASSIVE INCOME STREAMS, SUCH AS DIVIDENDS FROM STOCKS, INTEREST FROM BONDS, OR RENTAL INCOME FROM REAL ESTATE, OFFER A PARTICULARLY ATTRACTIVE AVENUE FOR BUILDING MULTIPLE INCOME STREAMS."

11. INVESTING WISELY: OFFERS GUIDANCE ON MAKING INFORMED INVESTMENT DECISIONS ACROSS VARIOUS ASSET CLASSES, INCLUDING STOCKS, BONDS, REAL ESTATE, AND CRYPTOCURRENCIES.

Investing wisely is a critical aspect of building wealth, achieving financial goals, and securing long-term financial well-being. This chapter explores the principles, strategies, and considerations involved in making informed investment decisions across various asset classes, including stocks, bonds, real estate, and cryptocurrencies. By understanding the fundamentals of investing and adopting a disciplined approach, individuals can navigate the complex world of investments with confidence and achieve their financial objectives.

Understanding Investment Basics:

Before delving into specific asset classes, it's essential to understand the fundamental principles of investing. Investing involves allocating resources—whether money, time, or effort—into assets with the expectation of generating returns or appreciation over time. Investors seek to grow their wealth by taking calculated risks and capitalizing on opportunities presented by various asset classes and investment vehicles.

Stocks:

Stocks, or equities, represent ownership stakes in publicly traded companies. Investing in stocks involves purchasing shares of a company's stock with the expectation that its value will increase over time, allowing investors to profit from capital appreciation and dividends. Stocks offer the potential for high returns but also carry higher risks due to market volatility and the unpredictable nature of individual companies. To invest wisely in stocks, individuals should conduct thorough research, diversify their portfolios, and adopt a long-term perspective to weather market fluctuations.

Bonds:

Bonds are debt securities issued by governments, corporations, or municipalities to raise capital. When investors purchase bonds, they are essentially lending money to the issuer in exchange for regular interest payments and the return of the principal amount at maturity. Bonds are typically considered safer investments than stocks, offering more predictable returns and lower volatility. However, they also tend to offer lower returns compared to stocks. Investing wisely in bonds involves assessing credit quality, interest rate risk, and maturity terms to build a balanced and diversified bond portfolio.

Real Estate:

Real estate investing involves purchasing, owning, and managing properties with the expectation of generating rental income, property appreciation, or both. Real estate offers the potential for attractive returns, tax benefits, and portfolio diversification. Investors can invest in various types of real estate assets, including residential properties, commercial properties, and real estate investment trusts (REITs). Successful real estate investing requires thorough market research, financial analysis, and property management skills to identify lucrative opportunities and mitigate risks.

Cryptocurrencies:

Cryptocurrencies are digital or virtual currencies that use cryptography for security and operate on decentralized networks based on blockchain technology. Bitcoin, Ethereum, and other cryptocurrencies have gained popularity as alternative investments offering the potential for high returns and portfolio diversification. However, cryptocurrencies are highly speculative and volatile assets, subject to regulatory uncertainty and technological risks. Investing wisely in cryptocurrencies involves conducting due diligence, understanding the underlying technology, and only investing what you can afford to lose.

Diversification and Risk Management:

One of the fundamental principles of investing wisely is diversification—spreading investments across different asset classes, sectors, and geographic regions to reduce overall risk. Diversification helps investors mitigate the impact of adverse events affecting any single asset or market segment and smooth out investment returns over time. Additionally, risk management strategies such as asset allocation, portfolio rebalancing, and dollar-cost averaging can help investors navigate market volatility and achieve long-term financial objectives.

Investment Horizon and Goals:

Investing wisely requires aligning investment decisions with one's investment horizon, risk tolerance, and financial goals. Whether investing for retirement, saving for a major purchase, or building wealth for future generations, individuals should tailor their investment strategies to match their unique circumstances and objectives. Short-term investors may focus on preserving capital and generating income, while long-term investors may prioritize growth and capital appreciation.

Due Diligence and Research:

Before making any investment decisions, individuals should conduct thorough due diligence and research to assess the potential risks and rewards. This involves analyzing financial statements, evaluating market trends, understanding industry dynamics, and assessing the competitive landscape. Additionally, seeking advice from financial professionals, such as financial advisors or investment managers, can provide valuable insights and guidance to help investors make informed decisions.

Investing wisely is essential for achieving financial success and building wealth over the long term. By understanding the fundamentals of investing, diversifying across various asset classes, conducting thorough research, and aligning investment strategies with one's financial goals and risk tolerance, individuals can navigate the complexities of the investment landscape with confidence and achieve their financial objectives. Whether investing in stocks, bonds, real estate, cryptocurrencies, or other assets, adopting a disciplined approach and staying informed are key to making informed investment decisions and securing a prosperous financial future. In the chapters that follow, we will delve deeper into the practical strategies, resources, and real-world examples that illuminate the path to investing wisely, empowering readers to take control of their financial destinies and achieve their long-term financial goals.

"WHETHER INVESTING FOR RETIREMENT, SAVING FOR A MAJOR PURCHASE, OR BUILDING WEALTH FOR FUTURE GENERATIONS, INDIVIDUALS SHOULD TAILOR THEIR INVESTMENT STRATEGIES TO MATCH THEIR UNIQUE CIRCUMSTANCES AND OBJECTIVES."

12. BALANCING WORK AND LIFE: ADVOCATES FOR MAINTAINING A HEALTHY WORK-LIFE BALANCE AND NURTURING RELATIONSHIPS AMIDST CAREER PURSUITS.

In the fast-paced world of modern society, striking a balance between work and personal life has become increasingly challenging. The demands of career pursuits, coupled with the pressures of everyday life, often leave individuals feeling overwhelmed, stressed, and disconnected from the things that truly matter. However, prioritizing a healthy work-life balance is essential for overall well-being, happiness, and fulfillment. This chapter explores the importance of nurturing relationships amidst career pursuits and advocates for maintaining a healthy balance between work and personal life.

Understanding Work-Life Balance:

Work-life balance refers to the equilibrium individuals seek to achieve between their professional responsibilities and personal commitments. It involves managing time, energy, and resources in a way that allows individuals to excel in their careers while also nurturing relationships, pursuing hobbies, and maintaining physical and mental well-being. Achieving work-life balance is not about perfect symmetry or equal allocation of time to work and personal life but rather about finding harmony and fulfillment in both domains.

The Importance of Nurturing Relationships:

Amidst the hustle and bustle of career pursuits, relationships often take a backseat, leading to feelings of isolation, loneliness, and disconnect. However, nurturing relationships—whether with family, friends, romantic partners, or colleagues—is essential for emotional support, social connection, and overall well-being. Strong relationships provide a sense of belonging, foster empathy and understanding, and enrich life with shared experiences, laughter, and love.

Quality Time vs. Quantity Time:

When it comes to nurturing relationships, quality trumps quantity. Spending quality time with loved ones involves being fully present, engaged, and attentive, regardless of the amount of time spent together. Whether it's sharing a meal, taking a walk, or engaging in meaningful conversations, the quality of interaction matters more than the quantity of time spent. By prioritizing meaningful connections and moments of genuine intimacy, individuals can strengthen relationships and foster deeper bonds with those who matter most.

Setting Boundaries and Prioritizing Self-Care:

Maintaining a healthy work-life balance requires setting boundaries and prioritizing self-care. This involves establishing clear delineations between work time and personal time, setting realistic expectations for workload and availability, and learning to say no to excessive demands or commitments. Prioritizing self-care activities such as exercise, meditation, hobbies, and relaxation is also essential for recharging energy levels, reducing stress, and nurturing overall well-being.

Creating Rituals and Traditions:

Rituals and traditions play a crucial role in nurturing relationships and creating a sense of connection and continuity. Whether it's weekly family dinners, annual vacations, or holiday traditions, these rituals provide opportunities for bonding, shared experiences, and cherished memories. By creating and maintaining meaningful rituals and traditions, individuals can strengthen relationships, foster a sense of belonging, and create a supportive and nurturing environment for themselves and their loved ones.

Flexibility and Adaptability:

Maintaining a healthy work-life balance requires flexibility and adaptability to navigate the ever-changing demands of career and personal life. Rather than striving for rigid balance, individuals should embrace the ebb and flow of life and adjust their priorities and commitments accordingly. This may involve reevaluating goals, reprioritizing tasks, and renegotiating boundaries as circumstances evolve. By remaining flexible and adaptable, individuals can navigate the complexities of work and personal life with grace and resilience.

The Role of Communication:

Effective communication is essential for maintaining work-life balance and nurturing relationships. Clear and open communication with colleagues, supervisors, and loved ones helps set expectations, establish boundaries, and address conflicts or concerns proactively. By expressing needs, sharing feelings, and seeking support when needed, individuals can cultivate understanding, trust, and mutual respect in both professional and personal relationships.

Finding Meaning and Purpose:

Ultimately, achieving work-life balance is not just about managing time or reducing stress—it's about finding meaning and purpose in both work and personal life. Meaningful work that aligns with personal values and passions can enhance overall well-being and fulfillment, while meaningful relationships provide support, connection, and a sense of belonging. By aligning career pursuits with personal values and priorities, individuals can create a life that is rich, meaningful, and deeply fulfilling.

Balancing work and life is essential for overall well-being, happiness, and fulfillment. Nurturing relationships amidst career pursuits requires prioritizing quality time, setting boundaries, prioritizing self-care, creating rituals and traditions, embracing flexibility and adaptability, fostering effective communication, and finding meaning and purpose in both work and personal life. By cultivating a healthy work-life balance and investing in meaningful relationships, individuals can create a life that is fulfilling, enriching, and deeply rewarding. In the chapters that follow, we will delve deeper into practical strategies, resources, and real-world examples that empower readers to achieve work-life harmony and nurture relationships amidst career pursuits, fostering a life of joy, connection, and fulfillment.

"BY CREATING AND MAINTAINING MEANINGFUL RITUALS AND TRADITIONS, INDIVIDUALS CAN STRENGTHEN RELATIONSHIPS, FOSTER A SENSE OF BELONGING, AND CREATE A SUPPORTIVE AND NURTURING ENVIRONMENT FOR THEMSELVES AND THEIR LOVED ONES."

13. OVERCOMING CHALLENGES AND RESILIENCE: EXAMINE COMMON OBSTACLES ON THE PATH TO SUCCESS AND STRATEGIES FOR BUILDING RESILIENCE AND PERSEVERANCE.

Life is filled with challenges, obstacles, and setbacks that can test our resolve and shake our confidence. Whether in pursuit of personal goals, professional success, or overall well-being, encountering difficulties is inevitable. However, it's how we respond to these challenges that defines our journey and shapes our outcomes. This chapter examines common obstacles on the path to success and explores strategies for building resilience and perseverance in the face of adversity.

Understanding Challenges:

Challenges come in many forms—personal, professional, financial, health-related, and more. These obstacles can manifest as setbacks, failures, rejections, or unexpected roadblocks that derail our plans and shake our confidence. Common challenges include fear of failure, self-doubt, lack of resources, financial constraints, time constraints, and external factors beyond our control. Recognizing and acknowledging these challenges is the first step toward overcoming them.

The Power of Resilience:

Resilience is the ability to bounce back from adversity, adapt to change, and thrive in the face of challenges. It involves harnessing inner strength, maintaining a positive outlook, and persevering in the pursuit of our goals and aspirations. Resilient individuals possess a growth mindset—they view challenges as opportunities for growth, learning, and self-improvement. By cultivating resilience, individuals can overcome obstacles with grace, courage, and determination.

Strategies for Building Resilience:

Building resilience is a journey that requires intentional effort and practice. There are several strategies individuals can employ to strengthen their resilience and persevere in the face of challenges:

1. **Cultivate a Growth Mindset:** Embrace challenges as opportunities for growth and learning. Adopt a positive outlook and believe in your ability to overcome obstacles and achieve success.

2. **Develop Coping Skills:** Build a toolbox of coping skills to manage stress, regulate emotions, and navigate adversity. Practice mindfulness, deep breathing, meditation, or other relaxation techniques to stay centered and focused.

3. **Seek Support:** Reach out to friends, family, mentors, or support groups for guidance, encouragement, and emotional support. Sharing challenges and seeking perspective from others can help alleviate feelings of isolation and provide valuable insights and advice.

4. **Set Realistic Goals:** Break larger goals into smaller, manageable tasks and set realistic expectations for progress. Celebrate small victories along the way and acknowledge your achievements, no matter how small.

5. **Learn from Setbacks:** Instead of dwelling on failure or setbacks, extract lessons and insights from your experiences. Use setbacks as opportunities for reflection, self-discovery, and growth. What can you learn from this experience? How can you use this knowledge to improve and move forward?

6. **Stay Flexible and Adaptive:** Embrace uncertainty and adapt to changing circumstances. Remain open to new possibilities, alternative solutions, and unexpected opportunities that may arise along the way.

7. **Practice Self-Care:** Prioritize self-care activities such as exercise, adequate sleep, healthy nutrition, and relaxation to recharge energy levels and maintain physical and mental well-being.

8. **Stay Persistent:** Perseverance is key to overcoming challenges and achieving success. Stay committed to your goals, even in the face of adversity. Keep moving forward, one step at a time, and trust in your ability to overcome obstacles and realize your dreams.

Real-World Examples of Resilience:

Throughout history, countless individuals have demonstrated remarkable resilience in the face of adversity. From entrepreneurs overcoming business failures to athletes rebounding from career-ending injuries, stories of resilience abound in every walk of life. These individuals serve as inspiring examples of the power of resilience to overcome obstacles, achieve success, and transform adversity into opportunity.

Overcoming challenges and building resilience are essential skills for navigating life's ups and downs and achieving success and fulfillment. By cultivating a growth mindset, developing coping skills, seeking support, setting realistic goals, learning from setbacks, staying flexible and adaptive, practicing self-care, and staying persistent, individuals can strengthen their resilience and persevere in the face of adversity. In the chapters that follow, we will delve deeper into practical strategies, resources, and real-world examples that empower readers to overcome challenges, build resilience, and achieve their goals with confidence and determination.

"RESILIENT INDIVIDUALS POSSESS A GROWTH MINDSET—THEY VIEW CHALLENGES AS OPPORTUNITIES FOR GROWTH, LEARNING, AND SELF-IMPROVEMENT"

14. CASE STUDIES: PRESENT REAL-LIFE SUCCESS STORIES ACROSS DIFFERENT PATHS, SHOWCASING DIVERSE TRAJECTORIES TO ACHIEVING FINANCIAL STABILITY.

In the pursuit of financial stability and success, individuals embark on diverse paths, each uniquely shaped by their circumstances, goals, and aspirations. Real-life success stories offer valuable insights into the strategies, challenges, and triumphs of individuals who have achieved financial stability through perseverance, innovation, and resilience. This chapter presents a collection of case studies highlighting different trajectories to achieving financial stability across various contexts and industries.

Case Study 1: From Rags to Riches

Sarah's journey to financial stability began with humble beginnings. Growing up in a low-income household, Sarah faced numerous challenges and setbacks. However, she was determined to create a better life for herself and her family. Through hard work, determination, and unwavering perseverance, Sarah pursued higher education, obtained a college degree, and secured a stable job in the tech industry.

Despite facing adversity and financial struggles along the way, Sarah remained focused on her goals and continued to invest in her education and professional development. Through strategic networking, mentorship, and seizing opportunities for advancement, Sarah steadily climbed the corporate ladder, eventually landing a leadership position at a prestigious tech company.

Today, Sarah enjoys financial stability and success, with a thriving career, comfortable lifestyle, and financial security for herself and her family. Her journey serves as a testament to the power of resilience, perseverance, and determination in overcoming adversity and achieving financial stability against all odds.

Case Study 2: Entrepreneurial Success

John's path to financial stability took a different route—he embarked on the entrepreneurial journey. After years of working in the corporate world, John grew disillusioned with the limitations of traditional employment and yearned for greater autonomy and fulfillment. Inspired by his passion for technology and innovation, John decided to take the leap and launch his own startup.

With a clear vision, strategic planning, and a relentless drive for success, John poured his heart and soul into building his company from the ground up. Despite facing numerous challenges, setbacks, and setbacks, including funding constraints, market competition, and technical hurdles, John persevered, learning from failures and pivoting when necessary.

Through persistence, creativity, and a commitment to excellence, John's startup gained traction, attracting investors, customers, and media attention. Today, John's company is a thriving success, with a loyal customer base, innovative products, and a growing team of talented professionals. His entrepreneurial journey serves as an inspiring example of the transformative power of passion, perseverance, and resilience in achieving financial stability and success.

Case Study 3: Real Estate Investment

Anna's journey to financial stability took a different path—real estate investment. After years of working in the corporate world, Anna sought to diversify her income and build wealth through passive income streams. Inspired by the potential for long-term growth and stability in the real estate market, Anna decided to invest in rental properties.

With careful research, financial planning, and due diligence, Anna identified lucrative investment opportunities in up-and-coming neighborhoods with high demand for rental housing. She purchased her first rental property, renovated it to attract tenants, and managed it diligently to ensure positive cash flow and tenant satisfaction.

Over time, Anna continued to expand her real estate portfolio, acquiring additional rental properties and leveraging financing strategies to maximize returns. Through smart investment decisions, proactive property management, and a focus on long-term growth, Anna built a diversified real estate portfolio that generates passive income and appreciates in value over time.

Today, Anna enjoys financial stability and security, with a steady stream of rental income, capital appreciation, and opportunities for future growth and expansion. Her success in real estate investment serves as a testament to the potential for building wealth and achieving financial stability through strategic investment in income-generating assets.

Real-life success stories offer valuable lessons and insights into the diverse paths to achieving financial stability. Whether through perseverance in the face of adversity, entrepreneurship and innovation, or strategic investment in income-generating assets, individuals can achieve financial success through determination, resilience, and strategic decision-making.

These case studies illustrate the transformative power of passion, perseverance, and resilience in overcoming challenges and achieving financial stability. By drawing inspiration from these real-life success stories and applying the lessons learned to their own lives, individuals can chart their own paths to financial success and fulfillment, realizing their dreams and aspirations along the way. In the chapters that follow, we will delve deeper into practical strategies, resources, and tools for achieving financial stability and success, empowering readers to take control of their financial destinies and build a brighter future for themselves and their families.

"REAL-LIFE SUCCESS STORIES OFFER VALUABLE LESSONS AND INSIGHTS INTO THE DIVERSE PATHS TO ACHIEVING FINANCIAL STABILITY."

15. CONCLUSION: SUMMARIZES KEY INSIGHTS AND ENCOURAGES READERS TO CHART THEIR UNIQUE PATHS TO SUCCESS, EMPHASIZING THE IMPORTANCE OF CONTINUOUS GROWTH AND ADAPTATION.

As we come to the conclusion of this journey through the realms of financial stability, career growth, personal development, and resilience, it's essential to reflect on the key insights gained and to reinforce the importance of continuous growth and adaptation in navigating the complexities of life. This final chapter serves as a culmination of the knowledge, strategies, and inspiration shared throughout this book, encouraging readers to chart their unique paths to success and fulfillment.

Reflecting on Key Insights:

Throughout this book, we've explored a myriad of topics—from financial literacy and investing wisely to overcoming challenges and nurturing relationships. We've delved into case studies of real-life success stories, examined strategies for building resilience and perseverance, and offered practical advice for achieving financial stability and personal growth.

Key insights gleaned from these discussions include the importance of:

1. **Financial Literacy:** Understanding the fundamentals of personal finance, budgeting, investing, and managing income and expenses is crucial for building a solid financial foundation.

2. **Investing Wisely:** Making informed investment decisions across various asset classes, diversifying portfolios, and prioritizing long-term goals are essential for achieving financial success and security.

3. **Overcoming Challenges:** Building resilience, perseverance, and adaptability are critical skills for navigating life's inevitable challenges and setbacks and emerging stronger on the other side.

4. **Nurturing Relationships:** Cultivating meaningful connections with family, friends, colleagues, and mentors is essential for emotional support, social connection, and overall well-being.

5. **Balancing Work and Life:** Prioritizing self-care, setting boundaries, and fostering work-life harmony are essential for maintaining balance, reducing stress, and achieving fulfillment in both professional and personal domains.

Embracing Continuous Growth and Adaptation:

As we conclude this journey, it's important to recognize that the pursuit of success is not a destination but rather a lifelong journey characterized by continuous growth, learning, and adaptation. Success is not static—it evolves over time as we evolve as individuals, as our circumstances change, and as the world around us shifts.

Embracing continuous growth and adaptation requires:

1. **Lifelong Learning:** Committing to ongoing education, skill development, and personal growth is essential for staying relevant, adaptable, and resilient in an ever-changing world.

2. **Flexibility:** Remaining open to new opportunities, challenges, and experiences allows us to adapt to changing circumstances and seize opportunities for growth and advancement.

3. **Resilience:** Cultivating resilience in the face of adversity, setbacks, and failures empowers us to bounce back stronger, wiser, and more determined to pursue our goals.

4. **Reflection:** Taking time for introspection, self-assessment, and reflection allows us to gain insights into our strengths, weaknesses, values, and aspirations, guiding our decisions and actions moving forward.

5. **Adaptability:** Embracing change, uncertainty, and ambiguity with a spirit of curiosity and adaptability enables us to thrive in dynamic and unpredictable environments.

Charting Your Unique Path to Success:

As you embark on your own journey toward success and fulfillment, remember that your path will be uniquely yours. There is no one-size-fits-all formula for success—each individual must chart their own course, guided by their passions, values, strengths, and aspirations.

Take inspiration from the insights shared in this book, but don't be afraid to forge your own path, experiment, and take calculated risks. Embrace failure as a natural part of the learning process, and view setbacks as opportunities for growth and self-discovery.

Above all, stay true to yourself, follow your intuition, and pursue goals that align with your values and aspirations. Success is not defined by external metrics or societal expectations—it's about living authentically, making a positive impact, and finding fulfillment in the journey itself.

As we conclude this journey through the realms of financial stability, career growth, personal development, and resilience, I encourage you to embrace the wisdom gained, cultivate a mindset of continuous growth and adaptation, and chart your unique path to success and fulfillment.

Remember that success is not a destination but rather a journey — a journey filled with challenges, opportunities, triumphs, and setbacks. Embrace each step of the journey, savor the moments of growth and learning, and celebrate your progress along the way.

May you embark on this journey with courage, curiosity, and determination, knowing that you have the knowledge, skills, and resilience to overcome any obstacle and achieve your dreams. Here's to a future filled with possibility, purpose, and prosperity.

"REMEMBER THAT SUCCESS IS NOT A DESTINATION BUT RATHER A JOURNEY — A JOURNEY FILLED WITH CHALLENGES, OPPORTUNITIES, TRIUMPHS, AND SETBACKS."

ABOUT THE AUTHOR

Armando Marichalar is a rising star in the world of literature, poised to make a significant impact with his unique voice, compelling storytelling, and insightful perspectives. Born and raised in a small town nestled in the heart of the countryside, Armando's passion for writing was ignited at a young age as he found solace and inspiration in the pages of books.

Armando's journey as an author began as a personal quest for self-expression and creativity — a journey fueled by a deep-seated desire to share stories that resonate with readers on a profound level. Drawing inspiration from his own life experiences, as well as the rich tapestry of human emotions and relationships, Armando weaves narratives that are both timeless and universal, capturing the complexities of the human experience with honesty, depth, and authenticity.

With a background in psychology and a keen interest in exploring the intricacies of the human psyche, Armando brings a unique perspective to his writing, delving into the depths of human emotion, motivation, and behavior with empathy, insight, and sensitivity. His characters are vividly drawn, multi-dimensional beings who grapple with love, loss, hope, and redemption, navigating the complexities of life with courage, resilience, and grace.

Armando's writing style is characterized by its lyrical prose, evocative imagery, and thought-provoking themes that resonate long after the final page has been turned. His stories are imbued with a sense of wonder, curiosity, and wonderment, inviting readers on a journey of self-discovery, introspection, and transformation.

As a new author in the making, Armando is excited to embark on this literary journey, eager to connect with readers from all walks of life and to inspire, entertain, and uplift through the power of storytelling. With a steadfast commitment to excellence, a passion for creativity, and a boundless imagination, Armando is poised to make a lasting impact on the literary landscape and to leave an indelible mark on the hearts and minds of readers everywhere.

In his free time, Armando enjoys immersing himself in nature, exploring new cultures, and seeking inspiration in the world around him. He believes in the transformative power of art, literature, and storytelling to inspire change, foster empathy, and unite humanity in our shared journey through life.

Armando Marichalar is a name to watch in the world of literature—a fresh voice, a bold talent, and a storyteller for the ages. As he embarks on this exciting new chapter in his journey as an author, the world eagerly awaits the stories that he will share and the impact that he will make on the literary landscape.

www.ingramcontent.com/pod-product-compliance
Lightning Source LLC
Chambersburg PA
CBHW070129230526
45472CB00004B/1480